# SOLIDS, LIQUIDS AND GASES

## By • THE • ONTARIO • SCIENCE • CENTRE

*Science Fair*

## PHOTOGRAPHS BY RAY BOUDREAU

KIDS CAN PRESS

First U.S. edition 1998
Text copyright © 1995 by The Centennial Centre of Science
and Technology
Photographs copyright © 1995 by Ray Boudreau

Published in Canada by
Kids Can Press Ltd.
29 Birch Avenue
Toronto, ON M4V 1E2

Published in the U.S. by
Kids Can Press Ltd.
85 River Rock Drive, Suite 202
Buffalo, NY 14207

Written by Louise Oborne and Carol Gold
Edited by Valerie Wyatt
Designed by James Ireland/Peter Enneson
Typeset by Archamedia

Printed in Hong Kong by Wing King Tong
Company Limited

CMC      95 0 9 8 7 6 5 4 3
CM PA   98 0 9 8 7 6 5 4 3 2

**Canadian Cataloguing in Publication Data**

Main entry under title:
Solids, liquids and gases

(Starting with science)
Includes index.

ISBN 1-55074-195-0 (bound)   ISBN 1-55074-401-1 (pbk.)

1. Matter — Experiments — Juvenile literature.  2. Matter — Juvenile
literature.  I. Boudreau, Ray.  II. Ontario Science Centre.  III. Series

QC173.36.S65 1995          j530.4'078          C94-932454-X

Kids Can Press is a Nelvana company

# Table of contents

# Balloon blow-up

You can blow up a balloon with your mouth. But here's a way to blow one up without any huffing and puffing.

## You will need:

- a balloon
- a small funnel
- a spoon
- baking soda
- vinegar
- a small juice or soda bottle

## What to do:

**1**. Stretch the balloon, so that it will be easy to blow up.

**2**. Use the funnel to put two large spoonfuls of baking soda into the balloon.

**3**. Half fill the bottle with vinegar.

**4**. Stretch the neck of the balloon over the neck of the bottle. (You may need an adult to help you with this.) Don't let any baking soda fall into the bottle.

**5**. Ready to blow up the balloon? Hold the balloon up so that all the baking soda falls into the vinegar in the bottle.

## What's happening?

When baking soda (a solid) and vinegar (a liquid) get together, they produce a gas called carbon dioxide. The gas takes up more room than there is in the bottle. So it blows up the balloon.

## Solids, liquids and gases

Everything in the whole world is made of tiny bits called molecules. How close together the molecules are and how they move is different in solids, liquids and gases. Get some friends together and act like a solid, liquid or gas.

Hold hands and stand as close together as you can — really squeeze together — and stay very still. You are acting like the molecules in a solid.

Still holding hands, spread out so you can move. Sway and walk so the group forms different shapes. Now you are acting like the molecules in a liquid.

Let go hands and spread out. Run around. Bump gently into one another. Now you are acting like the molecules in a gas.

# Rock candy

What's hard as a rock and sweet as candy? Rock candy! Ask an adult to help you mix a solid with a liquid to make some rock candy.

## You will need:

- a small saucepan
- 250 mL (1 cup) water
- 375 mL (1½ cups) sugar, or more
- a wooden spoon
- a glass
- a pencil
- a piece of clean cotton string

## What to do:

1. Ask an adult to boil the water in the saucepan and remove it from the stove.
2. Add the sugar to the water and stir. (Ask an adult to help you with this step, too. The water is very hot.)
3. When all the sugar disappears, stir in more. Keep adding a little at a time until you can see sugar floating in the water.
4. Let the sugar water cool a little. Then pour it into the glass.
5. Tie the cotton string around the pencil. Rub some sugar into the string, so that a few grains stick to it.
6. Drop the free end of the string into the sugar water. Rest the pencil on the rim of the glass.
7. Put the glass in a cool place, then don't touch the glass.
8. Wait a few days, then gently pull the string from the water. Taste the solid that clings to the string.

## What's happening?

The sugar didn't really disappear. Each tiny piece of sugar broke into smaller and smaller bits and spread out in the water. This is called dissolving. Because the water was warm, its molecules were spread far apart. There was room for the little bits of sugar to fit between the molecules. When the water cooled, its molecules moved close together again and squeezed the sugar out. The little bits of sugar stuck to the sugar already on the string and formed large chunks.

## What is a solid?

Solids are hard. They don't change shape easily. The molecules in a solid are tightly packed together and don't move.

# Magnet power!

Drive a car without an engine. There's no magic to it — just magnets.

## You will need:

- paper
- colored markers or crayons
- scissors
- adhesive tape
- a paper clip
- a large piece of light cardboard
- a small magnet (a fridge magnet will work)

## What to do:

**1**. On the paper, draw a car the size shown here.
**2**. Use the scissors to cut out the car. Color the car if you wish.
**3**. Tape the paper clip to the back of the cut-out car.

**4**. Draw roads on the piece of cardboard. Make sure the roads are wide enough for your car. Add some houses and stores.
**5**. Put the car on one of the roads. Hold the magnet beneath the cardboard, right under the car. Move the magnet to move the car. Can you steer it along the roads?

## What's happening?

A magnet is a special kind of solid that pulls metal objects toward it. Why? Because a magnet has an invisible force field that many metal objects just can't help following. Your car moved because the paper clip taped to it was following the magnet's force field.

## Sticking together

Collect some solids, including a penny, a nail, a ball of paper, an eraser and a button. Try picking up each with the magnet. Put the solids you can pick up in one pile and the others in another. What's different about the two piles?

# Ice fishing

Can you lift an ice cube out of a glass of water with a piece of string? No knots allowed! Sound impossible? Here's how.

## You will need:
- a small ice cube
- a glass of cold water
- a piece of string about 15 cm (6 inches) long
- salt

## What to do:
**1**. Put the ice cube into the glass of water. Wait until it stops bobbing.
**2**. Carefully lay one end of the string across the top of the ice cube.
**3**. Sprinkle some salt over the string where it touches the ice.
**4**. Slowly count to 10, then gently lift the string. If the ice cube falls, start all over with a fresh ice cube and clean water. Wow! You've caught an ice cube. But how?

## What's happening?
When you sprinkled salt onto the ice cube, the ice cube melted a little. A small pool of water formed on the top of the ice cube and the string sank into it. Then the pool of water froze, trapping the string.

## What is melting?

The molecules in a solid are close together and don't move. The molecules in a liquid are spread out and can move. When a solid gets warm enough, the molecules start to move and get farther apart. A solid turns into a liquid. This is called melting.

# Ice cream dream

Stir up a batch of old-fashioned ice cream — and change a liquid into a solid at the same time!

## You will need:

- 125 mL (½ cup) cold whipping cream
- 25 mL (2 tablespoons) white sugar
- a drop of vanilla
- a measuring cup
- a large Styrofoam cup, 300–350 mL (8–10 ounces)
- clean snow or finely crushed ice
- 60 mL (4 tablespoons) salt
- 2 stir sticks
- a small paper cup, 150 mL (4 ounces) (the ones that come from bathroom dispensers work well)

## What to do:

**1.** Mix the cream, sugar and vanilla together in the measuring cup. Chill the mixture in the fridge.

**2.** Fill the Styrofoam cup about one-third full with snow or ice.

**3.** Add the salt to the snow or ice and stir. (Mark the stir stick so you won't use it by mistake in the ice cream mixture.)

**4.** Pour enough cream and sugar mixture from the measuring cup to fill the paper cup three-quarters full.

**5.** Make a hole in the icy slush in the Styrofoam cup big enough for the paper cup. Add more snow or ice mixed with salt around the paper cup but don't let it get into the cream mixture.

**6.** Stir the cream mixture quickly with the clean stir stick. You will have to stir for quite a while, so you may want help.

**7.** As you stir, scrape around the bottom and sides of the cup to loosen any frozen pieces. Stop from time to time to let the ice cream mixture harden. In about 20 minutes the ice cream will be ready.

## What's happening?

You started out with a liquid mixture of cream and sugar. The crushed ice cooled the liquid into a solid as you stirred.

## What is freezing?

Liquids turn into solids when they get very cold. Why? Because the molecules huddle closer together and stop moving. This is called freezing.

# Water wonder

Look at the three containers. Which one has the most water? Read on to find out.

## You will need:

- 3 clear containers of different sizes and shapes (for example, a glass, a bowl and a salad dressing bottle)
- 2 measuring cups
- water
- food coloring
- a friend

## What to do:

**1**. Before your friend arrives, fill each container with 250 mL (1 cup) of water.

**2**. Stir a few drops of food colouring into each container.

**3**. Line the containers up on a table. Ask your friend to guess which has the most water and which has the least.

**4**. Empty the container your friend says has the most water into one of the measuring cups. Pour the water from the container with the "least" water into the other cup. Is your friend surprised?

## What's happening?

When you pour water into a container, it spreads out inside. If you have a small container, the water may fill it up. If the container is large, the water may only cover the bottom. So the small container may appear to have more water than the large one.

## What is a liquid?

The molecules in a liquid are loosely connected and can move around to fill whatever space they are in.

# Soap boat

Next time you fill up a bath or wading pool, try sending a power boat zooming through the water. You can use shampoo for fuel.

## You will need:

- a pencil
- scissors
- a piece of cardboard with a shiny surface (a piece of empty cereal box works well)
- a bath tub or wading pool
- shampoo

## What to do:

1. Draw a boat shaped like this one on a piece of cardboard. Make the boat larger, about the size of your hand.

2. Cut out the boat shape. Be sure to cut out a notch at the back.

3. Put water in a bath tub or wading pool. Wait until the water is still, then gently rest the cardboard boat on the surface with the shiny side down.

4. Put a small drop of shampoo into the notch at the back of the boat. Watch it go! Add another drop of shampoo when your boat slows down. How long can you keep your boat going?

## What's happening?

Water molecules like to stick together. They hold on to one another and form a kind of "skin" over the surface of the water. You can't see or feel this skin, but it's there. Shampoo "unzips" this skin. The boat moves along like the pull on an opening zipper.

# Empty glass trick

Is an empty glass really empty? If you said "yes," you're in for a surprise…

## You will need:
- a paper towel
- a glass

## What to do:

1. Stuff the paper towel tightly into the bottom of the glass. It should stay there even when you hold the glass upside down.

2. Fill a sink with water.

3. Turn the glass upside down. Hold the glass very straight and plunge it into the water.

4. Slowly count to 10. Lift the glass out of the water without tipping it.

5. Pull the paper towel out of the glass. Is the paper still dry?

## What's happening?

The paper in your glass stayed dry because water couldn't get into the glass. Why not? Because the glass was already full of air.

## A huff 'n puff trick

Fool your friends with this balloon trick. Push a deflated balloon into a soda bottle. Stretch the open end of the balloon back over the bottle's mouth. Challenge a friend to blow up the balloon. Why won't it work?

## What is a gas?

Your bottle and glass are full of air — a mixture of gases. Smell the gases in the air. Stick out your tongue and taste them. Most gases don't have a smell or a taste, and most are invisible. But we know they are around us because they take up space, just as the air in your bottle and glass does.

# Strong air

Turn a glass of water upside down and the water will pour out. Or will it? Try this to find out.

## You will need:
- a glass half filled with water
- a piece of stiff, flat cardboard

## What to do:
**1**. Put the cardboard over the top of the glass.

**2**. Hold the cardboard tight against the glass.

**3**. Turn the glass upside down over a sink while holding the cardboard in place. Keep the glass straight.

**4**. Take your hand away from the cardboard. Surprised?

## What's happening?
Air pushes up, down and sideways on everything it touches. This pushing power is called air pressure. The air pushed up on the cardboard more than the water and air inside the glass pushed down. This kept the water from falling into the sink.

# Summer frost

Frost in summer? Sound impossible? Try this and see for yourself.

## You will need:

- a spoonful of Epsom salts (available in drug stores)
- 50 mL (¼ cup) very hot water
- a glass pie plate or baking dish

## What to do:

**1**. Pour the Epsom salts into the hot water. Stir until the salts disappear.
**2**. Pour a thin layer of the salt water into the glass dish.
**3**. Set the dish outside in the sun or in a warm place and leave it for an hour. Where did the frost come from?

## What's happening?

You didn't make real frost. You made a sparkling pattern that looked like frost. How? The Epsom salts separated into tiny pieces that fit in between the water molecules. As the water evaporated, the little pieces of salt were pushed back together. They stuck to tiny bumps and scratches in the glass. The pieces can only fit together in certain ways. This produces a pattern that looks like frost.

## What is evaporation?

As the water warmed up, it turned into a gas called "water vapor" and floated away in the air. This change from a liquid to a gas is called evaporation. The salt did not evaporate — it was left behind on the bottom of the dish.

# Indoor rain

Have you ever been stuck inside on a rainy day? Where does all that rain come from? Try making some rain in your own kitchen to find out.

## You will need:
- a large metal spoon or soup ladle
- a kettle one-quarter filled with water
- oven mitts

## What to do:
1. Put the spoon into the freezer to cool it. Leave it there until it's ice cold.
2. Ask an adult to boil water in the kettle.
3. When the water is boiling, put on your oven mitts and remove the spoon from the freezer.
4. With the oven mitts on, hold the cold spoon in the white cloud coming from the kettle's spout. In a few seconds you'll see "rain" falling from the bottom of the spoon.

## What's happening?
When the cloud of air and water vapor touches the spoon, it cools suddenly. Cooling makes the molecules of air in the cloud scrunch closer together, which pushes out the water. This is called condensation. The water falls. Presto! Indoor rain.

## Outdoor rain
When the sun warms up the water in rivers, lakes, oceans and even puddles, tiny droplets of water evaporate. This water vapor rises into the sky and forms a cloud. Cold air up in the sky can't hold as much water as warm air can. So droplets form around little specks of dust in the air. Thousands of these droplets clump together to form a raindrop. Time to get out your umbrella!

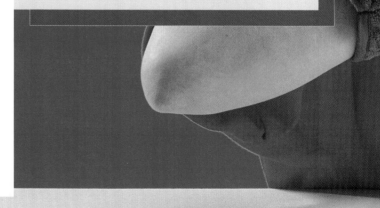

## What is condensation?

When warm, moist air meets a cool surface, tiny droplets of water form. We call this condensation. Try breathing on a cold window. The water in your warm breath condenses on the cold window.

# Raisin race

Open a soft drink and you'll hear a fizz and see bubbles. There is a gas dissolved in the liquid! Use the gas to give some raisins a ride.

## You will need:
- a clear glass
- ginger ale or another clear soft drink
- several raisins
- a spoon

## What to do:

1. Carefully pour the ginger ale into the glass. If you tip the glass and pour the ginger ale gently down the side, you will keep more of the fizz in the liquid.

2. Drop two raisins into the ginger ale. Watch them race up and down.

3. Use the spoon to remove the raisins. Squeeze one of them to flatten it. Now drop both raisins back into the ginger ale. Does one raisin go up and down faster than the other?

4. Put a bunch of raisins into the ginger ale and watch them race.

## What's happening?

The raisins rise on a bubble elevator. Where do the bubbles come from? A soft drink has a special gas called carbon dioxide dissolved in it. A machine pumps the gas into the soft drink at the factory, then the lid is sealed. When you open the drink, the hiss you hear is the gas escaping.

As the gas comes out of the spaces between the molecules of liquid, it sticks to the raisins. When there are lots of bubbles, they lift the raisin to the surface. There the bubbles break and the raisin sinks again.

# Ooblik

Make some ooblik and you'll discover that things aren't always what they seem. Is this melt-in-your-hand marvel a liquid — or a solid?

## You will need:
- 2 or 3 sheets of newspaper
- a box of corn starch
- a small cake pan
- a pitcher of water (add some food coloring, if you wish)
- a spoon

## What to do:
1. Spread the newspaper out on a table.
2. Put some corn starch into the pan and add some of the water. Stir.
3. Keep adding water and stirring until the mixture is as thick as mayonnaise. You've made ooblik. Make more ooblik until you have a layer 1 cm ($\frac{1}{2}$ inch) deep.
4. Lift up a spoonful of ooblik and pour it back into the pan. Does it pour?
5. Slap the pan of ooblik with the flat of your hand. Does any splash out?

6. Scoop up a handful of ooblik. Roll it around between your hands to make a ball. When you think you've made a ball lift your top hand up. What happens? **Don't pour the ooblik down the drain.** Scrape it into the garbage.

## What's happening?
Corn starch is made of millions of tiny particles. When you add water to the starch, the particles float freely, keeping themselves spaced evenly apart. Imagine the floating starch particles are like a school group going through a doorway. If everyone walks in an evenly spaced line, the group passes through easily. But if everyone tries to push through at once, the group gets jammed in the doorway. The same thing happens to ooblik. When you move the ooblik mixture slowly or gently, as when you stir it or pour it, the starch particles can slide easily past one another. The mixture acts like a liquid. When you try to move the mixture quickly or push on it hard, such as slapping it or squeezing it, the starch particles get pushed together and the mixture acts like a solid.

# For parents and teachers

*Experimenting is a good way to introduce young children to principles of science. The activities in this book are designed to show that matter is everywhere, that matter comes in three forms (solid, liquid or gas) and that these forms can be changed by such factors as temperature or pressure. Here are some ideas to extend the activities in the book. These questions invite children to develop theories and test them through open-ended experimentation.*

## Balloon blow-up

What is a solid? A Liquid? A Gas? Have an around-the-house (or school) hunt and list all the solids, liquids and gases you find.

## Rock candy

What other solids dissolve when placed in a liquid? Fill several glasses with water and put a different solid into each. Try salt, chocolate drink powder, rice, instant coffee, coffee beans. Which solids dissolve? How are they similar?

## Magnet power!

In most solids, molecules are aligned in random directions. In a magnet, all the molecules are lined up in the same direction. To make a simple magnet, rub a paper clip in one direction along a magnet about 50 times. Can your magnet pick up other paper clips or objects?

## Ice fishing and Ice cream dream

Why was salt used in these two experiments? Salt lowers the freezing point of water. When salt mixed with the wet surface of the ice, the resulting salt water wasn't cold enough to stay frozen. In the process of melting, it actually loses heat and gets even colder. Try putting a thermometer into a glass of ice and adding salt. Does the temperature drop?

## Water wonder

Do different liquids move in different ways? Pour water from one glass into another. How long does it take? Test the pouring time of other liquids, such as cooking oil, liquid soap, molasses and corn syrup. The size of the molecules and how much they cling together (their viscosity) determine their flow speeds.

## Soap boat

Fill a glass with water. Does the water bulge over the top? The molecules of water cling together, almost like a "skin" over the surface, keeping the water from spilling over. This is called "surface tension." Drop in coins, one at a time. How many can you add before the surface tension breaks?

## Empty glass trick

Which takes up more space — warm air or cool air? Blow up a balloon then deflate it. Put the mouth of the balloon over the neck of an empty bottle. Set the bottle in a pan of hot water. Wait for a few minutes. What happens to the balloon? Replace the hot water with ice. What happens to the balloon now?

## Strong air

Try the same experiment using a piece of window screen instead of cardboard. Is air pressure still strong enough to keep the water in?

## Summer frost

Hold an evaporation race. Ask a child to make a water droplet evaporate. Try blowing on it, fanning it, or drying it with a hair dryer or lamp. Which method is fastest? Why?

## Indoor rain

Where else does water condense? Put a small potted plant into a plastic bag and seal it. Water evaporates from the plant's leaves and condenses on the bag.

## Raisin race

A soft drink contains gas. What other foods contain gases? Make some muffins. The holes inside are caused by carbon dioxide that formed when baking soda was combined with acidic ingredients in the batter and heated. Do other foods have these gas holes?

## Ooblik

What helps a liquid change to a solid? Try heating some ooblik. In a saucepan combine 250 mL (1 cup) corn starch, 500 mL (2 cups) baking soda and 375 mL ($1\frac{1}{2}$ cups) water. Cook until clumps form, pour into a bowl, cover with a damp cloth and cool. Has the ooblik changed? Use it like clay.

# Words to know

**air:**      a mixture of gases, mainly nitrogen and oxygen

**air pressure:**      the force that air places on anything it touches

**condensation:**      the process by which a gas changes to a liquid

**dissolve:**      to make a solution by mixing a substance into a liquid

**evaporation:**      the process by which a liquid changes to a gas

**freeze:**      to change a liquid to a solid by cooling it

**gas:**      a form of matter whose molecules are not connected to one another and move randomly in space. Oxygen is a gas.

**liquid:**      a form of matter that can flow freely and take on the shape of its container. Water is a liquid.

**matter:**      any substance that takes up space and has weight. Matter has different forms — it can be a solid, a liquid or a gas.

**melt:**      to change a solid to a liquid by heating it

**molecule:**      the tiniest particle into which a substance can be broken without changing it chemically. All matter is made up of molecules.

**solid:**      a form of matter that has a shape of its own. A rock is a solid.

# Index